Becoming The Drunk Mom

Copyright and Legal Bullshit

Printed in the United States of America

First Printing, 2016

ISBN 978-1-365-49189-4

The Drunk Mom
PO Box 66
Decatur, AR 72722

www.TheDrunkMom.com

Forward and Thanks

This book is written like a conversation. A conversation where I do all of the talking, of course, kinda like we're at a party where I'm the really prematurely drunk one (but still slightly coherent) and I'm telling you stories about my life and how I got be where I am today.

But not boring stories, these are stories of pain and struggle and heartache but also laced with humor and lessons and inspiration too. What good is a lesson, after all, if you don't learn from it AND then share it with other people so it can help them too?

I'm ignoring the "writing rules," partly because of my rogue personality and partly to give my high school English teacher the finger for being a stone cold bitch and ignoring my potential as a writer. And I also don't want to put you to sleep, so there's that.

Ignoring grammar and proper sentence structure and all of that bullshit and just giving you the stories in the most raw, unedited way possible, feels awesome. Because (see, you aren't supposed to start a sentence with the word "because") I want you to feel like I'm with you, sharing my life with you and hopefully inspiring you, making you laugh and making you cry a little bit too.

Being brave and honest and sharing all of the irrevocable details of my life with the world has been terrifying and cathartic and freeing… and fucking terrifying. But it's helped me somehow grow as a human too and realize that every single thing I've been through has helped me become the person I am today- honest, imperfect and real (and awesome… most days and an asshole some days).

I hope reading this book gives you what you need in this moment to somehow be a better human than you are right now too, or just makes you giggle until you wet your britches. Whatevs.

Humongous thanks to my parents, for giving birth to a fucking legend ☺ and for being super supportive of every crazy idea that I've ever had… ever. Even the really stupid ones.

Thanks to my kids and husband for letting me share our lives so openly, in an effort to help other people realize that they are not alone and are, in fact "normal", even amidst dysfunction and heartbreak.

Thanks to my little brother for being my playmate (and my punching bag) in childhood and a huge supporter in adulthood.

Thanks to every single fan, follower and supporter who encouraged me, supported me and helped me get to this point and will continue to do so in the future. You have a solid place in my entourage and I can't wait until we can gather around a beachside campfire together and share a toast to us for being epic and changing the world, one laugh at a time.

Thanks to Nikki Elledge Brown for being awesome and brainstorming with me and texting with me when I feel like a lunatic (more than I'd like to admit).

Thanks to Courtney Cope for supporting and mentoring me in this crazy new space I'm in.

Thanks to Shonte' Jovan Taylor for seeing the comedian in me years before I started this journey.

Thanks to Tara Kennedy Kline for epic chats and a long distance friendship based on humor and booze.

Thanks to Marie Forleo whose journey, vision and creation of BSchool has forever changed my life and introduced me to the **most** incredible, loving, ambitious people on the planet.

Thanks to everyone who has somehow led me to where I am now, bad or good. You know who you are.

And finally, thanks to Oprah... because everyone in the universe needs to thank Oprah for everydamnthing they ever do. She's the original badass and has showed all of us with her own life, that you can turn a shit situation into an awesome one and create whatever life you want, whenever you want, with no excuses.

Smooches, Amy

Damn, It's Cold

I decided to grace the world with my presence in the spring of 1980 in Anchorage, Alaska. You're welcome! My parents were young, free spirited, pot smoking kids who had been together since my mom was fourteen years old, my dad fifteen… and now, here I was, crashing the party a few years later!

I'm told that I attended their wedding in-utero which, in my opinion, is the best way to attend a wedding unless, of course, you're of legal drinking age.

The fact that I was born in Alaska is hilarious because, you see, I cannot stand the cold. I hate it. If it's not seventy degrees outside, I am just not a happy girl. Lucky for me, before I reached my first birthday, we moved to Northern California. Yes, we still had winter and sometimes even snow, but compared to Alaska… come on! In my heart, I'm originally a California girl.

Most of my great childhood memories took place in California, and some not so great ones too. I have memories starting around age two, playing in my little splash pool in our apartment front yard, listening to airplanes flying overhead with my friend Megan, who had really long hair. I remember my first favorite song was "Eye of the Tiger," (I still love that shit! It's my go-to feel good song when life starts to get tough.)

I even remember the day my brother was born in November 1982, because we went to the hospital to see him and I got into trouble for playing with the remote on my mom's hospital bed. It's funny the things that stick with you- and I totally understand now, that most people do not have memories this early… I'm weird like that and have shit- for-brains for a memory now (I recently forgot exactly how many kids we had for just a minute when someone asked me). So there. We're even!

My parents were awesome parents. We were always taking trips and doing fun things and they would always have parties and get-togethers with friends and take us along. That was the norm back then for us. Nobody had babysitters- everyone we knew took the kids along. The parents would play (AKA, drink like fish) and the kids would play. I was almost always the one "in charge" of the little kids and babies because I LOVED them.

When I was eight, we lived in a little town called Rough and Ready (I know... weird). My brother and I used to build forts in the trees and underbrush in our yard and play outside for hours. We really loved it there.

We would hide in a flowerbed full of flowers and watch the hummingbirds get scary-close to our heads and we'd laugh and laugh and laugh. We would take long walks with our dogs down the dirt roads. One time we were all walking our dogs and the dog my dad was walking saw a rabbit or something and took off running like and Alaskan sled dog. My dad was the sled. I'm not sure if he had the leash wrapped around his wrist or he just didn't want to let the dog go, but all we could see was a dog running with everything he had in him and a cloud of dust behind him where my dad was supposed to be walking. It was like something from a Roadrunner cartoon and it was hilarious... well, for us. My dad was scraped up from head to toe and super pissed at that dog.

California is beautiful but notorious for droughts in the summer and also for the fires that those droughts bring, which sucks for people who live there. My dad was out of town one weekend in September so my mom, my brother and me were chillin' around the house, building forts and shit and like we normally did. We got the news that there was a wildfire fire spreading closer to where we lived and as the sky got darker and the smoke got heaver, eventually, some firemen came to our house and we were asked to evacuate our home as quickly as possible.

My mom grabbed pictures, baby books, packed an overnight bag, packed the dogs- the necessities. I grabbed my hamster. My brother grabbed a few of his toys because at age six, that's what's important. My mom had just bought me an antique typewriter- the kind that comes in its own carrying case that I loved so much. I wanted to take it but we didn't have room in the truck, so I typed my dad a letter with it, telling him that we were going to a friend's house because of the fire. I left that letter on my mom and dad's waterbed for him to read when he got home (this was back in a world before cell phones kids, so we had no way of telling him anything).

My dad eventually found us at my aunt's house after he wasn't allowed to return home because all of the roads were blocked off. I don't recall how many days we were away, but it felt like forever when we were finally allowed to return home as a family, to see what the damage was. We headed down our road, around the corner and looked on top of the hill but our home was absent from the place it was supposed to be. I'll never forget hearing the cries of my parents as they saw everything that they had worked so hard for in ashes. "It's all ashes." My dad cried. That was the first time I remember seeing him cry.

We kept on, driving up our once familiar driveway that now seemed to be so foreign. No buildings, no trees, no brush where we built forts... nothing. We sifted through the rubble to salvage anything that we could... that will stay with me for the rest of my life. I found a couple of the little ceramic decorations that used to be on my dresser, along with a tin that kept my coin collection that had now melted slightly. I still have those things.

Obviously, my dad never got my letter. I envisioned it burning to the ground along with everything else we owned. The only thing left standing was our chimney.

We were homeless, as were many others. We were in a big gymnasium where the Red Cross was gathering information and taking donations for all of the displaced families like ours. I remember my dad saying "we have each other and that's all that matters." He was right.

I don't remember much after that about what we did in the following weeks, I think because it was so traumatic for all of us. My brother and I pissed the bed for months after that, (actually I think my brother was a bed wetter until he was like 12) which seems like a really weird, embarrassing reaction, but my understanding is that it's normal. My next memories are the best ones- of us living in a small travel trailer at a campground by a lake- Camp Far West Lake.

My parents bought the trailer and we set up a semi-permanent camp. As an adult now, hearing of a family living in a trailer at a campground sounds horrible. Nightmarish even! As a kid though, for my brother and me, it was the time of our lives! We swam in the lake every day, caught lizards and rode our bikes with all of the other kids who lived there. My parents eventually bought a boat and we'd ski and tube and kneeboard. We'd go tent camping and have parties… it was the LIFE for us, all of us.

We became closer as a family in that time than ever (that tends to happen when you share less than four hundred square feet of space). Having lost everything and being forced to see what was *really* important, our lives were forever changed and I think looking back, changed in a good way.

The kindness of strangers is what stood out to me the most then, even as an eight year old kid I saw it. People donated money, clothes, kitchen utensils, blankets, furniture, toys and everything in between for us. I still have a Christmas ornament that someone donated to us that I still I hang on my tree every year. It's my favorite ornament because it's a reminder of that time when we had nothing and people were there when we needed help the most. It's my reminder that people are inherently good.

The power of our senses tied to a memory is amazing. To date, I still cannot smell smoke on a summer day, even twenty-eight years later, and not have a memory or some reaction of this traumatic time, however brief.

Helping people is a pillar of my life and always has been. You understand why now, right? I always wanted a career in "helping people" I just never knew what that meant. Likely because the internet wasn't around yet and I was terrified to be seen by people… but we'll talk about that later.

Always the New Kid

Even before the fire, we moved around a lot when I was a kid. My dad was a manager for a tire franchise and he went where they needed him. I ended up being "the new kid" at five, maybe six different schools, in my lifetime. For a kid who was already painfully shy, I panicked at the thought of having to even say my name in class, let alone stand up and tell people about myself. It was absolutely terrifying.

My hands would sweat and my heart would race and my face would turn the color of a beet. I hated being seen in class, or anywhere, for that matter.

I was born with a sense of humor and a desire to entertain my parents (and they always laughed at me when I was being a character), so I eventually found that being funny was my key to fitting in quickly. Telling little jokes or making silly comments was my in with new friends and a way to cut the tension of meeting new people. By moving around so many times in my childhood, it started this cycle of comedy for me. Even in book presentations and show-and-tell, when I HAD to get in front of the class, which again, I hated, I'd get a laugh or two. I was my thing and it grew as I grew.

When we moved to Decatur, Arkansas (population 1,367) to be near my grandparents when I was thirteen, I fit in quickly because the school was a tiny-ass, country high school and I was the girl from California (and probably also because I was getting boobs, let's be honest). I found my quick wit in high school because I dressed the way I wanted to dress and acted the way I wanted to act… and got bullied a bit as a result but I learned a new skill from it.

High school is where I first learned to tell people to "fuck off" and I did it with gusto. I was done with taking peoples' shit. Before long, those people were my friends and I was playing on the basketball team, being voted into the homecoming court and "class favorite" (and almost "class clown" a few times).

Decatur was, of course, a country town. There wasn't shit to do. The closest town with as much as a move theater was a good half hour away (still is to this day). For fun, the kids would drive dirt roads and drink. They'd have bonfire keg parties in cow pastures. They'd ride four wheelers. They'd hang out in the one parking lot in town big enough to house the dozens of trucks that would park in a circle so everyone could "hang out".

Basically drinking, "hanging out" and having sex was the town hobby. Every once in awhile, someone would haul a giant hay bale into the middle of the four-way stop in the night and light it on fire… that's about the extent of the entertainment.

Not for me though. I was sheltered as fuck. My dad was raised as an abused kid his whole life and had an extremely rough childhood. While he didn't abuse us (I'm so grateful to him for breaking that pattern), he was strict and I was his oldest child so I wasn't allowed to go out or date or anything without the onset of a million rules. Even spending the night with friends took an act of congress.

I landed my very first serious boyfriend at age fourteen, who ended up being a much more long term fixture in my life than I'd planned. I didn't want to "go out with him" but I didn't want to hurt his feelings by saying no when he asked me, so I thought I'd let him hang around for awhile. That tactic did not work. We ended up "in love", or whatever you want to call it in those early teen years. I even wore the letterman jacket and the class ring wrapped with thread so it would fit my finger. We'll call him "Dick" (name disguised, but eerily accurate).

When I finally got the guts to tell my dad about my boyfriend who wanted me to go to prom with him, he insisted that they have a "talk". Oh Goddamn. I was terrified but it went well and I got to go!

After that, I finally got to start going out on dates with my boyfriend and that was my one "out". I had a curfew, of course, but I was getting more freedom than I had in my whole life! Dick, who was two years older than me, eventually graduated high school and went to a local college. He was always skipping classes in favor of being with me (naturally, because I was the shit!) and decided he didn't want to go anymore. When his parents kicked him out of his house for dropping out, my parents, to my utter shock, let him stay at our house. Nice gesture… but horrible decision.

Things were always tense between us and got worse as time went on and I was dragged into his jealous fits. He always wanted to know who I was talking to, why I was getting dressed up, where I'd been, why I wanted to be with friends instead of him. The beginnings of what I now know to be abuser patterns. But I was a 17 year old girl in high school, I had no clue.

HOLY SHIT

It was December of my senior year. My period was late, like, really late. I was throwing up during my high school basketball practice every day and the smell of, well just about everything made me run to the nearest bathroom, sink, trash-can or whatever would hold vomit. So there I stood, in my bathroom, 17 years old, holding a positive pregnancy test that I'd bought secretly on a trip to the grocery store with my mom.

"Oh shit". I said, tears running down my flushed face. "Oh my God"!

We were shocked but we shouldn't have been. Truth is that we were lucky that it hadn't happened sooner. I somehow knew that I would be a young mom and now were going to be parents.

The "birds and bees" discussion, well, I learned the way most kids learn about those things- from school friends. We knew better, we knew we needed to be careful, but of course, it would never happen to us.

Terrified to tell my parents, I went over possible scenarios in my head but could never actually say the words. Eventually my mom guessed what was going on based on my avoidance of her, my horrible mood and likely the fact that I was a puke factory every single day. You can only claim you have the flu for so long, right?! She and my dad were shocked but more supportive than I could have ever imagined.

Muddling through my senior year of high school, no longer focused on my future, I was instead planning baby names and doctor appointments. While my friends were shopping for Calvin Klein jeans and Doc Martins, I was shopping for stretch pants and baggy shirts to hide my baby bump at school and at my job at the local convenience store.

At 5'7" and 120 pounds, my belly didn't show for a long time because I was super in shape thanks to rigorous basketball practices. I only confided in my best friend, at the time and asked her not to tell anyone that I was, in fact, pregnant. My graduating class had less than thirty people in it, so you can imagine the speed of my news when she told one of her friends and that friend told another and so on and so on. It was like a cross between a fucked up game of telephone and an episode of Jerry Springer.

That Bitch.

I was "the pregnant girl" in school. Yay. Good thing I had *some* level of popularity so I wasn't a laughing stock. People were actually really supportive and my new group of friends, well they were high achieving, straight A, Christian good girls… sooo opposite me, but I adored them. I was like a fat, black stallion in a flock of white sheep. Even still, they loved me and supported me and made me feel cared for in a time when I was terrified, uncertain and feeling out of place. Senior prom time came around and I announced that I wasn't going because… well, maternity prom dresses weren't exactly all the rage back then.

But the amazing friends I had presented me with a gift one day. As I opened it, I realized it was material and ribbon with a pattern for a maternity formal dress, to be made especially for my huge measurements. It was unconditional friendship that I had never really experienced before.

Prep time… I read the parenting books. I took a parenting class (you know, the one where you carry around the robotic baby that cries all of the fucking time? I did that 5 months pregnant in high school.) Thank God I made a 98% in that class. I'm sure I was the envy of my classmates who were planning for their senior trip and college!

I became closer to my mom than ever during my pregnancy. She went to every appointment and organized our baby shower. She really showed me what it meant to be loved in those months. Knowing what I know now about being a parent, I can see how much support and grace and love she showed us during that time in my life.

She was thirty six years old when I made her a grandma. The same age I am at the time of writing this book. I hope my son has more sense than I do. (I need to hurry up and publish this motherfucker so he can read it and hopefully soak in some wisdom… maybe.)

She and my dad could have easily kicked me out, shunned me, been disappointed and gave me a huge lecture. They never did. I can't remember a time when my parents complained about anything. They told me they'd be there for us, they loved us and showed us that ever day. Even when things got terribly tough, they stood by me. Eighteen years later, nothing has changed and I could not be more grateful.

My baby daddy and I moved out on our own across town, close to my high school, when I was about five or six months pregnant. Looking at that house today, it's possibly the smallest shithole you've ever seen, stuck right in the center of about twelve chicken houses (because… Arkansas) but to me, it was my beginning… a sign of my new life as an adult and as a mom.

"Give Me the Juice!"

At what was to be my last OB appointment, my doctor was eager to schedule an induction because I was a few days over my due date (I didn't know enough yet to tell him to fuck off at the prospect of intervening in a perfectly natural process). I spent the day before what was to be our son's birthday, trying not to be nervous, relaxing and mentally preparing for the big day.

Dick spent the night before our appointment, playing in a softball game but I chose to stay home because it was late July in Arkansas, sweltering and my ankles were already puffy and gross. I spent the last night of my life as a childless young woman on the couch by myself watching a movie-Dumbo, to be precise, the part where the mom, Mrs. Jumbo, sings "Baby Mine" I cried and cried.

We were in bed, trying to sleep when at about one in the morning, I felt the first contraction. Holy shit! This was going to happen even before we expected. This wasn't like you sometimes see in movies where women say "ooh, I think that was a contraction… maybe? And she's all giggly and excited and shit." This was hard and more painful than I could have ever imagined.

An older friend of mine said that contractions were like the worst gas pains you have ever experienced. She was not wrong but maybe could have used a few expletives in that description. Like "hey, it's going to feel like someone is running your guts through a fucking food processor and a bus is trying to drive out of your asshole and all things neighboring."

We rushed out the door, bags in hand calling family to let them know it was time. Before I could even get to the truck, there was another contraction that almost brought me down in the front yard like I'd been hit in the ass with a tranquilizer dart. The contractions started about four to five minutes apart and moved quickly to three minutes apart.

We got into the truck; ready for the thirty minute drive to the hospital... at least *I* was ready. Dick forgot to get gas on his way home from the stupid softball game so we had to go to the Goddamned gas station before leaving. I wanted to rip his pecker off and beat him with it (BTW, a **little** impossible, if you get my drift)!

I must have had two or three more contractions while he was filling up. I felt like my insides were being pulled out of my ass. My grip was firm on the passenger door, begging him to hurry up.

Asshole.

When we finally arrived at the hospital, and even though I'd already pre-registered, we spent time doing more paperwork, because I was clearly in a physical state that allowed me to think clearly! Ugh! It was so hard to resist throat punching the lady at the desk but I could barely breathe or stand up as it was, so a physical altercation was OUT.

Someone finally lackadaisically got me up to the Labor and Deliver floor. She handed me what looked like a twin sized sheet with some strings hanging off of it to somehow maneuver onto my huge body that I could no longer see half of. I went into the bathroom with this "apparel" and couldn't even stand up, let alone figure out how to assemble it into clothing. I remember holding onto the handicap railing by the toilet thinking "I know I wanted a drug free experience, but if this is just the beginning of labor and I can't hack it now... I'm getting the juice."

I told my mom when she got there, shortly after (and thankfully helped me navigate this stringy sheet situation) "I want an epidural now". This was more than I had bargained for so early on in the labor experience. This was stupid. I had nothing to prove. Give me the JUICE!!

I laid there in the hospital bed with my parents and little brother (and I'm sure baby daddy was there too but I don't really remember his presence) by my side for what felt like hours, writhing in pain. In reality, it was only a few minutes that had passed. The nurse said she'd be in to check me soon, like it was no big deal. No one really took me seriously when I told them how much pain I was in. Now maybe it was because I was a teenager, maybe because I was a first time mom, maybe both. They thought I was being a weenie. I am many things but a weenie is **not** one of them.

Out of nowhere, I felt this overwhelming urge to push. So I did. It was like the biggest shit I've ever taken, times six-hundred. The pressure was so intense; I made that "I'm taking a really big poop" face, where your mouth gets all distorted and weird. I think my mom recognized it. The nurse came into the room, lifted the sheet that was over my body and said something like "don't push, I can see the head".

No shit, lady.

The nurse had a broken arm in a sling so she did her best to wheel me down to delivery with her good arm, running my bed that I was still clinging to for dear life, into the wall a few times on our way. My doctor wasn't available so they called in another but he wasn't there yet either.

I did not care. This kid was coming out and I was totally fine with it. "Don't push, don't push!" the one armed nurse yelled to me.

I wanted to tell her to go fuck herself.

Now, I'm not a doctor, but when a baby wants to come out of your vagina and your body is designed to push said baby out of said vagina, there is not one iota of a shit that you can do about it, except maybe stress over the fact that people are telling you not to push! Not helpful.

The doctor arrived just in time to catch, so a few drug free pushes later and a bit of screaming because my hoo-ha felt like it was on fire, and I was a mom.

Welcome to motherhood, bitch! Buckle up.

Bretley was born at 3:05am on July 24th 1998.

Two months out of high school, I squeezed an 8 pound, 10 ounce baby boy out of my vajay-jay in record time. I fell so deeply in love in that moment and knew that I would do absolutely ANYTHING for that kid, and I meant it. Yes, I was young and naïve, but I knew in my gut that I would protect him and love him forever. There is no feeling stronger than the instinct of love and protection for your child. It was instant for me.

I stayed up all night holding him and staring at my nose on his face, even after everyone had gone home. I wouldn't let the nurses take him to the nursery. I talked to him, kissed his face at lease a thousand times and we watched Scooby-Doo together. It was just he and I together in our hospital room. A foreshadowing of what life would be like in the near future.

The first diaper of his that I changed, he shot a stream of piss all over the wall. That was my first lesson of many more to come: cover the winky quickly or risk getting shot.

I married Dick five months later, because that's what you're "supposed to do", at least according to lots of judgmental religious people and some of his family members. I will never forget when one man I didn't even know told me "this isn't the way the good Lord intended it", when he learned that I was pregnant but not married. The pressure was immense so I did what I thought was best and what I was "supposed to do" for my son. Not really knowing I had another choice.

Bret was five months old when our elaborately planned wedding took place. My parents rented the Mildred B Cooper glass chapel in Bella Vista, Arkansas on New Years Eve. They bought me a gorgeous white dress with the long-ass train and veil for the candle light ceremony. They rented a hotel banquet room for the reception, bought me a cake to die for that had dozens of roses on it, the limo, the wedding party attire… everything.

The night before the ceremony, my mom asked me if I was sure about marrying Dick. I was not. I knew in my heart this wasn't the thing I really, deeply wanted but I did promise to give my son the best life possible and my parents had already dumped thousands of dollars into this shit-show called a ceremony. The guilt of *not* going through with it and the embarrassment of telling everyone I'd changed my mind was too much for me to take. I was getting married. To Dick.

It was a gorgeous, evening ceremony and everything about the wedding itself was beautiful and perfect; the groom was the only thing that wasn't right.

Our wedding night was spent with him drinking too much champagne at our reception and going to bed early, while I spent the night hanging out with my friends and family. How romantic, right? I don't even think we had sex and if we did I don't remember which should tell you everything you need to know. It was not anything like I thought my wedding night would be. At all.

A Dick for a Hood Ornament

Not long after there were rings on our fingers (that I bought alone, by the way), shit got real, real quick. He was constantly jealous and always making comments, asking way too many questions when I did anything. "Where were you, who were you with, why did you take so long, who are you painting your nails for, who are you trying to impress wearing that?"

All of my friends were gone because it took so much time to explain a play by play of my time away, it was no longer worth the effort to go anywhere with them. I was isolated, with the exception of my parents who lived nearby. I went to my parents' house when things were too intense, which was a lot.

I'll never forget the times Dick physically restrained me so I couldn't leave and the way he'd get insanely jealous over trivial things. The way he'd inquire over and over again if I was cheating on him, even though I rarely left the house except to go to work and my parents'. The emotional abuse and belittling that took such a huge toll on my once solid self confidence was brutal.

I justified it away, telling myself this was normal. It was not.

Dick would take my keys when I tried to leave the house, trying to escape his madness. He'd taunt me with them and argue and argue and argue for hours on end. There was no escaping it. I'd end up so pissed off because I couldn't leave the room or the house, or do anything, except cry and take it until he was done.

One day, knowing the routine quite well and in an ingenious moment of foresight, I put my spare key in my glove box. As expected, we were in a heated battle, he held me down yelling in my face. I escaped him and ran to my car, locking the doors behind me (yes, these were the days before key fobs). He held up my keys as if to say "ha, ha... you can't leave".

I'll never forget the look of shock on his face and what must have been the look of complete satisfaction on mine, when I started my car and pulled out of the driveway. In a very, trailer-trash moment; he ran beside me and jumped on my hood, but I didn't stop for quite awhile. I fantasized about flooring it and running his ass over as I drove down the country highway. I had a Dick hood ornament and I liked it. I liked it a lot!

I just could not imagine my son being witness to this bullshit through the years. And there was no end to Dick's behavior. It actually got worse once he started drinking.

One of the last times we fought, the time that made me realize I was done, started at a Christmas party for his job, he picked up hard liquor, which sent read flags flying everywhere in my head like rebel flags at a redneck convention. I knew what was to come. I begged him to leave with me. He wouldn't. He got drunk and we ended up fighting all the way home. Forty-five minutes of him cussing me, calling me every name in the book and trying his hardest to make me feel less than- and it worked.

Some people can drink and be happy and silly or maybe even just get annoying and talk all fucking night. He was an angry, mean drunk. It brought out the very worst in him, which was more apparent by the day.

I walked into our house in tears and tried to go into the spare bedroom to get away from him. As I closed the door, he shoved it open and grabbed me. I tried to kick him off of me, losing my heavy platform shoe in the process. I walked over to the bed and as I turned toward him he picked it up and threw it at me, striking my face. He said the over-handed throw was an accident. It didn't hurt in that moment like I thought it would because apparently, adrenaline makes you a motherfucking superwoman.

The night ended with severely damaged sheetrock as I threw every single trophy he'd ever earned THROUGH the wall, trying to hit him to keep him away from me. My only regret is that he was able to dodge most of them.

Thank God my son wasn't there.

I went to the doctor the next day, because adrenaline can't last forever. My jaw hurt like Hell, to the point that I couldn't open my mouth and there was a bruise where the shoe hit me. That didn't hurt as much as the shame of answering the question "what happened?" to the nurses and doctors. It was unbearable to my pride as a strong, young woman.

How in the Hell did I get here, in a doctor's office for THIS?

I'd like to say that was the last time I put up with his bullshit and that I was gone forever but it took me some time to realize I couldn't force this to work for anyone. Not even my beautiful baby. Although it was scary and I felt ashamed and stupid, that was the first, best decision of my life, as a woman and as a mother, to walk out of that door for the last time. It was a huge weight off of my shoulders signing divorce papers. I was free. Well, sort of free.

I didn't ask for anything from our home in the divorce. Every kitchen utensil, every piece of furniture (except my gigantic bed that I bought), everything stayed. I even left behind some of Bret's old baby clothes and memorabilia. I knew he would battle me every step of the way so I let it all go. All I wanted was our freedom. That ended up being too much to ask for too.

When I started dating again, not long after I filed for divorce, my date was driving me home to my parent's house. To my complete shock, there was a car in the driveway with its lights off. Dick was sitting, waiting for me to return. I was afraid.

I asked my date to keep driving past, so he did. Dick followed behind us for miles and miles and miles. He tried to pass us, got really close to our bumper, honked, swerved and flashed his lights. I really thought he likely had a gun and was going to kill us. By the grace of God my date had a cell phone and called the police. They set up a roadblock in my small town but Dick likely saw it and turned before they could get him. It was a surreal experience when I realized the level of instability I was dealing with.

I divorced Dick for the same reason I married him- for my sweet, blue eyed, blond headed baby boy. I didn't want my son to be subject to the physical and emotional abuse that I was going through. Not ever. But I couldn't keep him from it because of nothing more than DNA.

Bruises Heal, Emotions Notsomuch

I was gone but not okay. My son was still small when we moved in with my parents and my divorce was final within 30 days, even though Dick threatened to refuse his signature on the papers. Thank GOD I had the strength to get the heck out when I did.

In my mind and in my heart, it was over forever. But the effects of that six year relationship would linger for YEARS. I started to believe that I was undesirable, damaged goods, not worthy, all of the things he'd told me. Looking back on pictures of myself at age twenty, I was freaking adorable. But inside, I was a wreck and my self worth tanked.

This period of my life was the first time I ever experienced depression and thought about suicide… and I thought about it often. I would mentally plan my own funeral until an image of my son would run through my mind. What would his life be without me in it? The fact that he would end up living with his psychotic father was enough to keep me above the dirt.

Bruises from physical abuse go away in time. Emotional and verbal abuse helped put me on a path of some horrible choices in men. Every wish I ever made on a star or on birthday candles at that point in my, life was for nothing more that "to be happy," and at that time, I thought that level of happiness required a relationship.

I was so desperate for happiness and affection and love. God knows I didn't love or respect myself at all for choosing a partner who was so mentally unstable. I also didn't want my son to grow up without a father figure in his life and I didn't feel like I was enough as a human, let alone a mother with dual roles, so I jumped right into the arms of someone I worked with. In retrospect, this guy was a total douche bag. He was married and wanted a divorce from his wife.

I was the bridge he needed to get from A to B; he was the confidence boost that I needed to feel alive and worthy again. It was a match made in Hell and doomed from the beginning. But I didn't know that then.

Just like they always do, the unresolved issues that I had in my marriage, appeared like magic in this relationship too! I didn't get it at the time, but this is just the way the universe works. You can never escape the lesson and until you learn it. That little son-of-a-bitch will just keep showing up in your life in different situations and different people until you finally GET IT.

And I didn't get it. At all. Not yet, anyway.

I'm a slow learner, but I was catching on to the whole "loving myself and knowing what I'm worthy of" thing. That was a key in my journey to finding happiness. It came first on my twenty first birthday when instead of my boyfriend taking me out to drink and have fun, we went to *his* favorite shithole dive bar and I ended up being *his* designated driver, taking his drunk ass back home. Happy twenty-first birthday to me, right?!

I could explain in great detail the crap relationships I've been in, but it gets redundant. Even I get sick of remembering. I wish I could get selective dementia... I'd pay for that shit. I'll give you the short version: Low self worth, settle for way less than I know I deserve, decide I have a low tolerance for bullshit. Leave. Repeat.

I wouldn't say these relationships were all in vein. Although I would never want to live through them again, I can look back and clearly see how they made me a better person. Trial by fire, ya know? Some of them opened my eyes to what I did not want, like the guy who climbed into my kitchen window drunk when I didn't answer my doorbell. Some opened my eyes to what I did want, like the guy who was super responsible, had a job and actually kept his house clean. Each of them put me one step closer to my dream of happiness and for that, I'm so grateful for every Dick, drunk, selfish ass-wad and horny prick that I momentarily shared my life with. So a big thank you to them... and in some cases, fuck you.

Sixteen Years a Slave

Despite my many, many repeated courses in Life Lessons 101, especially in the relationship sector, I was a good mom to my son and I never broke my promise to love him and care for him. I felt incomplete as a human so I'm sure I could have been more, but I gave him all I had. We spent time together and he was the focus of my whole world. Most of the decisions I made, in the end, came down to what was best for him. I did everything as best as I possibly could throughout my son's life. I didn't want to be a "teen mom statistic".

Statistics said as a teen mom and now as a single mom I should be on government assistance and not be successful. That he would end up incarcerated and we would live in poverty. I said bullshit! I wildly protested those statistics by doing everything I possibly could to be a responsible, amazing mom at any cost. I worked my ass off, striving for perfection but rarely (or never) quite reaching it.

We took trips together, read books, sang songs, played games. I listened to him tell his stories and jokes, even when they made no sense or when I would've rather shoved a pencil in my ear than hear how he could count to one-hundred… again. I went to football. And baseball, and basketball. And was the team mom. All of that shit that you're "supposed to do". I did that for him because he deserved to have the best and all I could provide him was at least one great parent whose world was built around him.

Many times I overcompensated for Dick's lack of presence in my son Bret's life. He would be the dad of the year when a new girl entered the picture, then disappear for a few weeks or months, then come back, then disappear. I call it "the girlfriend effect". Those moments also came with Dick taking me to court for no reason, just to impress his girlfriend and act like I was the one responsible for him being shitty human. It "wasn't his fault". Narcissism, it was amazing.

Even in those moments, I tried to push a relationship between Dick and our kid, but I learned quickly that you can't force someone to be decent or loving or unselfish. There was never a good relationship between the two of them, which is so sad for everyone, especially my son.

There was even a time when Bret would pull his own hair out in one spot, leaving it bald; I assume out of the stress that his father would put him through. One Thanksgiving, Dick had been absent for months and out of nowhere, called the night before the holiday, telling me that he'd be at my house in the morning to get our son. I told him no, we'd already made plans with my family and he cussed me and argued and fought and threatened and recorded our phone calls- swearing he would call the police.

At one point he called 10-15 times in a row when I wasn't home and left horrible messages because I didn't answer (obviously).

"I know you're therrrrre. You'd better pick up this phone or things are going to get real bad." (Translation: REAL BAD is redneck for really bad).

"Pick it up. I know you're listening so pick it up right now. I guess I'll have to take you back to court. Why are you being such a bitch?" he'd say.

He'd park outside of our home and videotape us. He told my son when he was only six years old "I'm going to have your mom arrested and thrown in jail." My poor kid.

The worst part was that I was not legally allowed to protect my son. Dick took me to court a couple times and threatened at least fifty other times, trying to get me arrested for contempt of court because I'd try to intervene in his acts of terrorism. Truly, it was terrorism. I should have called the police every, single time he made a scene but I was ashamed. Had I done that though, I might have been able to better protect Bret from his own father. But then again, he may have taken it out on Bret. At least I would have had documented proof, but was it worth the price?

The one time I did call the police, I understand he did have to go to court but I'm not sure what his punishment was. Clearly it wasn't enough to make him stop his ridiculous bullshit.

I would have done anything to free my kid from this man's torture. I offered to stop child support if he'd sign over his parenting rights. He wouldn't do it. He was so bitter and so angry; I guess he thought the torture was worth the $300/ month in child support to him. He would constantly say that he wanted a paternity test because our son had blonde hair and blue eyes, just like my dad, and we both had dark hair and dark eyes. I told him to set a paternity test up but he never did. He chose to bring it up dozens of times instead and talk about how Bret wasn't his.

I did my best to explain things in a way that Bret could understand, even though I couldn't understand it myself.

My hands were tied because, as judges and attorneys told me, "he hadn't broken the law where Bret was concerned" and he was "allowed visitation" and "I couldn't force him to visit his son". It was the biggest joke of a system I've ever seen, and there we were trapped in the middle of it for what would be the next sixteen years. Sixteen years of torment. Sixteen years a slave that would turn out to cause so very serious consequences later for my son.

It's a Girl!

When Bret was four, I remarried. We were a happy little family of three. Bret had a good stepdad who taught him to ride a bike and hang out with him like guys do. Bret started kindergarten and before long, we had a new, amazing change.

"What should we name your sister, Bret" I'd ask.

"Mike Wyzowski" he would say, as serious as he could be. His obsession with Monsters Inc. bled into our baby naming sessions.

I was ecstatic to be having a baby girl. I loved my son but there was something amazing about knowing that we'd get to do dresses and pink and hair bows and girl stuff. I started a corporate job while pregnant which I wasn't thrilled about it but we just couldn't make it on one income so I did it.

I found a local midwife that we met with and I immediately fell in love with the idea that I could have my baby at home, with natural methods with no poking or prodding. No people treating me like I had some weird, unnatural condition and no one-armed nurse barking at me and running me into walls. Sign me up!

I went into labor around 9pm on July 11th while at dinner at my mom's house with Bret. Baby girl decided to make her debut in an Arkansas thunderstorm. I called our midwife, drove myself home and prepped for the birth.

In a home birth, you have to buy all of these supplies like plastic sheets, bed pads, iodine, herbs for healing and rubber gloves. It's very empowering to have control over how your experience feels and the way your baby enters the world. It was for me anyway.

Our midwife arrived, Bret was asleep, my parents got there and my sister in law was on her way. I sat on the bed contracting like crazy with my mom and midwife standing by me and others just a room away. I had apparently lost all control in my nether-regions because as I sat there waiting for the next contraction, a loud fart just slipped right out with no warning at all. When people are gawking at your hoo-ha like a whack-a-mole game, farting in a room of people who are expecting to witness a miracle is a wee bit embarrassing.

I'd like to say the embarrassment stopped there. Alas, as I pushed and pushed and pushed, I heard a loud "snap" and sadly, sprayed the fuck out of my midwife with Niagara-force amniotic fluid when my water broke. I'm fairly certain I didn't apologize in that moment because... well, I was busy.

Thunder shook the house, wind howled and it was dumping rain... and then... fucking dark. The power went out. Baby girl was born minutes later by candlelight in what seemed like a magical moment for me. I didn't care one bit about power. I wasn't afraid at all... of anything. I was so prepared and so excited to meet this new little soul. I was in the zone and on July 12th at 12:13am she was born, weighing nine pounds even. She didn't even cry that much for the first couple of days of her life. She was gorgeous and perfect and my heart doubled in that moment.

That was the start of our new family. We were all so very happy, I found my happy. We named the new baby girl- Dezirae, not Mike Wyzowski, to Bret's disappointment. And I apologized to my midwife for the womb-juice shower.

After Dezi was born, I went back to work when she was only three weeks old because I had to. She stayed with a family member who ran an in-home daycare. It was heartbreaking and I cried at my desk all day long and then I'd finally stop and then people would come by my desk to see pictures of the baby... I'd cry again.

I'd also have to get a set of keys from security (a team of men) twice a day to go into the medical room and pump breast milk for her. I hated it. I just knew the whole damned building could hear the humming of the breast pump. Awkward.

Dezi grew to be the most kind-hearted, loving, funny, friendly kid I could have asked for. Truly, all kids are a blessing (most days), but I think The Universe knew that I needed a sweet little girl in my life. It was so right and we all adored her (still do!).

We bought a little house near my parents' and spent most of our time renovating before we moved in. I painted Dezi's room in pastel blocks and Bret's in Blue with motorcycle border. The house was located near a chicken farm and also near a Little Debbie bakery plant. Half of the time you'd step out onto the front porch and it would smell like cookies, the other half of the time it would smell like chicken shit. You'd always hope for the cookies.

The kids had a yard, Bret played sports, Dezi was a beauty pageant natural… things were good. But… alas, I realized that I'd settled again and I felt ignored in my marriage and again I felt like such a hopeless loser. Two marriages, two kids and divorced in my mid twenties.

Right after that marriage ended, I wish I could have checked some kind of life road map or crystal ball or something. I struggled hard. It wasn't like he was a horrible person or anything. I just didn't feel like he was the right person for me. He was husband of the year compared to Dick. That made it easy to re-unite a few times but we just couldn't make it work. I dipped back into depression briefly but made a very conscious decision that I was not going to wallow again, as much as I could help it. I was going to accept things as they were right now, in this moment. Not wishing, not waiting for a partner to do fun things, not settling for less than I deserved, dammit!

I was finally free. I was divorced again but this time felt like a big shift. I knew that I was free to make whatever decisions I wanted to make in my life. In fact, I wanted to paint my front door red for the longest time but my ex never liked the color red; so as a symbol of my new found freedom and, let's face it, an act of pure rebellion, I got the reddest fucking paint I could find and painted that door with such joy that I thought my heart would explode.

This was my house now. My HOUSE and my LIFE and I was no longer under the control of anyone. Yesssssss!

And with that house and that freedom life came a mortgage to handle on my own and sole responsibility of everything. I got a new job at that same corporation that fed my self worth some more and led me to great people, friends and bits of confidence.

That job ended up directly linking me to a huge promotion in the Wal-Mart corporate marketing department, on their events team. My team was responsible for organizing the huge events like shareholders and manager meetings for thousands of people.

I met celebrities like Queen Latifah, Wee Man from Jackass, LL Cool J, Shaq (he is scary eeenormous!), Gretchen Wilson and my personal favorite, Bob Barker. And one of the highlights of my freakin' life, I got to sit front row with my kids and watch Keith Urban perform. Sexy. As. Fuck. I almost got to meet him but I blew my chance because I wanted to finish my job. That'll teach me to be a hard worker!

Another huge highlight of that position was being able to put my mom and kids in the front row of the Eagles concert. My kids had no clue who in the Hell they were watching but wondered why Nana was crying over them. It was a big deal.

Little did I know that my life was going to change in even bigger ways…forever, in every possible way that it could from that one job!

As Comfortable as Cactus Underwear

I worked forty hours a week, sometimes sixty or more hours a week when we had big events or I had to travel. I was mom, dad, maid, chef, nanny, doctor, breadwinner, lawn care technician and still tried to squeeze friendships and being a human in there sometimes too. All moms can relate to this feeling whether they have a job or not.

Half the time we could have baled our yard for hay because the grass was so long, laundry seemed to breed while we were away, we had hamburger helper for dinner and the TV was afternoon entertainment but we were happy.

Like every other single parent in the world, there was a lot of pressure on me. Some of it was self induced, some was from societal expectations. It's the feeling of "what will people think of me, I have to do more, be more, have more." I started to lose sight of that happiness and loneliness and the feeling something was missing started setting in.

Most weekends that the kids were gone I would lay on the couch watching T.V. and sleeping from Friday night to Sunday morning. I was a recluse. I went through a period when even walking into the break room at work caused severe anxiety. Interestingly enough, I even realized at one point that I hadn't danced for years because I always felt like everyone was watching me, judging me and criticizing me. I sat out. I denied myself joy. I hid. Friends would ask me to go out to clubs and parties. If I did go, I'd sit in one place… never dancing or having fun.

In reality, I knew this wasn't healthy. It was something that I had to overcome to remain sane so I made the decision (which was so scary to me at the time) and I started going out every other weekend with friends instead of my standing date with my couch. At first it was about as comfortable as cactus underwear, just walking into a room of people was HARD, let alone a bar or club where people watch you DANCING. I later learned that this is called Social Anxiety Disorder, likely as a result of emotional trauma and maybe even hormonal imbalances and who knows what other bullshit contributed.

I learned to dance again, it was terrifying. Whiskey helped… a lot. Two drinks and I was ready to hit the dance floor. Five or six drinks and I'm dancing like fucking Madonna in "Vogue". I had a blast. So much so that every other weekend, I'd throw on my black leather pants, glittery eye shadow, stilettos and party girl attitude and we'd hit a club or two and dance until we were sweating like crazy and our legs were about to buckle.

I'm no psychologist, but I think I was living out the teen years that I never had. I wasn't the girl who got to go to parties or drink or do anything in high school, remember? And now we all know what my extracurricular activities *were* in my senior year, so this was the moment in life that I had fun and partied, trying to find some sort of alignment and balance, if such a thing exists.

Being a single mom was good, but tough.

There were times that I had to heat the house with the oven because we were out of gas for the heater and I couldn't afford to pay the bill to have it turned back on. There were times that I had to make the choice between groceries or the cable bill so we'd watch the same movies over and over for a few months. I remember specifically, putting the kids to bed and curling up on the couch to watch J Lo in "Monster in Law" about ten times or so. I learned how to strategically overdraw my checking account so as to incur the fewest overdraft fees possible when payday was a bit too far away.

It sucked at times, but we made it somehow.

Woo-Woo and Woo-Hoo!

Once my mom said something about me going out a little bit too much, I decided to just enjoy life without partying so much. You know… you might be in danger of a real problem if your family of beer drinkers, who could probably fund an international space station with their aluminum can refunds, thinks you're drinking too much.

Once I dropped the party girl act, I started exploring spirituality a bit more. I didn't have God fed to me in a box (AKA organized religion) at all as a kid. We didn't pray or really talk about God much as a family. I never even stepped foot in a church service until I was 22 years old. I appreciate that as an adult now because it led me to think for myself and explore without barriers on my own beliefs.

God was real though, I always had a strong sense of that. And I always felt deeply connected to nature and trees and animals. I was such a sensitive, dorky kid. One of my most prized positions was a bible for children that my grandma gave me as a gift when I was about three or four. It came in a shiny, wooden box that had a picture of Jesus on the front.

I treasured that thing. It was sacred to me for some reason… which is weird since I had no concept of religion. It was one of the things I grabbed when our house burned down. I always grabbed it first when I moved.

As an adult I later found out from my mom, that thing I treasured, that symbol of God to me… was fucking stolen from a hotel by my grandma. For GOD sakes! How funny is that!? Good thing I learned that God wasn't in a single place or a single thing or I may have been devastated!

I found a little Wicca shop not far from where we lived and bought a book with magic spells for fun. I flipped to a page that was for finding happiness and finding your true love, so I thought "eh, what the Hell?" I lit a white candle, wrote out some shit and sent it out to the Universe to handle. "Bring me Mister Right"! This was my first experience in exploring what I lovingly call the "woo-woo" side of myself and I loved it.

I found tarot and palm readings and psychics and metaphysical stuff. It fascinated me and opened up a whole new world of possibility and things I didn't know but felt like they were so 'slap your forehead' obvious.

I also decided that my lucky number, twenty three was my sign from the universe that things were on track. March twenty-third is my birthday so any variation of that, especially 323 is awesome. I started seeing it everywhere and I started paying attention.

The most depressing holiday for single people, Valentines Day, was coming soon. I booked a trip for myself, my eight year old and my three year old to go to Mexico after I got back from my company's upcoming meeting. We were going to have a little family vacay, no man needed! I wanted to give my kids life experiences NOW. I didn't want to wait "until". Until I had more money or until I had a man or until things were more stable or until they were a bit older... their childhood, our lives, were happening now and godammit I was going to be happy and embrace it!

It takes guts (or pure insanity) to travel internationally with small children alone. Looking back, I'm not sure what in the actual fuck I was thinking taking an eight and three year old out of the country alone, but I booked the trip on pure naivety. It was going to be awesome. We were so excited to swim with dolphins and snorkel and sail... yay, beach!

At work, it was time for our big corporate shindig in Kansas City, MO in the dead of winter. Now, if you haven't been to KC, MO in January... just fucking... don't. It was bone chillingly cold and windy as Hell. So, naturally, I warmed up with nightly whiskey after dinner since I didn't have my kids and I was working my rear off all day long.

While at dinner with a co-worker one Wednesday night, I met a group of people from all over the country who were also there to work for our meeting. What would happen next would change everything. There, through some mutual work friends, at The Quaff Bar and Grill, I noticed that a dude at our table kept staring at me. But it wasn't that kind of stare where you look up and catch them, and they immediately look away. You know that stare… every woman knows that stare.

His stare lingered for much longer. I initially thought "awe, Hell, another perve"… but there seemed to be a super kind, generous and giving side to him with everyone at our table whom he knew… and he shared a picture of his daughter with everyone. I assumed he was married and didn't think much more about it.

We were with a big group of fifteen or more people at our table and we were all drinking and having fun getting to know each other. I'd had several Crown and Cokes which means the witty, funny and sassy me comes out to play- understandably irresistible to the guy across the table.

We all drank and talked and laughed, then paid our tabs and walked back to our respective hotels, which were spread out around the city, as a big group (reminder… it was cold as FUCK!). The dude and I were walking along with the crowd dwindling. In time, and as fate would have it, it was obvious that we were at the same hotel. We got into the elevator- it went up and up stopping at each floor. Less people… less people… just the two of us.

"What floor are you on?" He said

"Eight." I stammered. Half hammered from the Crown and Cokes I'd thrown back.

"Me too" He said.

I'm sure at this point my mouth dropped onto my work boots, although I was too drunk to notice it. My mind is racing (as much as it possibly can at this moment) "Holy fucking shit! What are the chances?! But… married guy. Not doing that again!"

The elevator stopped and we got off (of the elevator… get your mind out of the gutter you freak!). His room was to the right of the elevator, mine to the left. But, like a gentleman, he walked me to my room. We exchanged pleasantries and I blurted out "Wanna see a picture of my kids?"

My foggy, drunk mind is thinking 'Jesus Christ Amy, that was forward', but he agreed and came into my room (again… get your mind right you horny ole weirdo!).

I showed him my kids' picture on my nightstand and he cooed about how cute they were. We ended up sitting on the bed talking. I put drag racing on the T.V. because back then I was into that kind of thing and it dulled the awkward silence.

He smelled so freaking good. He was tall and he had on this massive black leather jacket that must have weighed more than me. He was in security back then so I felt super safe walking downtown with him. There was definitely a connection for me instantly.

We talked awhile and in my daze, I boldly asked him about his life and it turned out… Chris was divorced and single. I'm sure my eyes got big when that little snippet came out. And before long I was learning much more about him, like what a fantastic kisser he was. I was done. In that moment, I knew this was something big (just stoppit).

"What's your last name" I asked him.

"Wright" he said.

His name was Chris Wright.

Holy shit… I asked for Mr. Right and got Mr. Wright. The Universe has a sense of humor.

History in the Making

This isn't a Harlequin Romance novel (it totally could be though!), but after that first night, we spent the next three weeks of our nights together and in passing throughout the day.

He did things that I'd never experienced before (yes… mind-garbage, in that way too) like turning up the thermostat before he left each morning because he knew I would be cold if it was below 72 degrees. He left me notes on the nightstand and even some that led me around my room like a little treasure hunt. He took me on an official date and held doors, pulled out my chair, told me that I looked pretty. He bought me gifts. He would give me his jacket when I was cold… which, hello? January in Kansas City, remember?! He walked on the sidewalk, nearest the road "just in case".

His appearance and experience, well let's just say he was not someone that you'd willingly fuck with in a street brawl. I always felt so safe with him.

I. Was. Hooked. Fast. And I didn't want to be. I wanted to be cool and wise and not have this boy drama again. But damn.

Chris lived almost exactly one thousand miles away from where I lived. We both cried on the day we had to leave because we knew this part of our amazing journey was coming to an end. I was heartbroken. He was too but we were going to stay in touch and see where things went. I had other things to focus on now- a vacation with my kids to get ready for. Passports and suitcases ready, we're wheels-up headed to Cozumel, Mexico.

I hope that my kids will say to this day that it's one of the best memories of their childhood. It certainly was for me and it gave me more confidence as a mother and a capable adult. We had a blast for a week together playing at the beach, eating nachos and cheeseburgers every day, dancing and playing.

My daughter, Dezi threw up red slushy all over the patio at the Dolphin experience... an experience it was! But I handled it and we still got to kiss a dolphin, a dream of mine.

Chris and I continued talking daily, even while I was in Mexico getting to know each other better and not wanting this "thing" we started to end. Hello $800 international cell phone bill! Holy shit!

Things with Chris fell apart within a few months, as many long distance things do. Ten days before my birthday, he called to tell me he had decided that he was going to pursue a relationship with someone he had been with before. He thought that the distance between us was too great and there was no solution in sight. I was devastated and pissed that he gave up and rejected me. But life went on. I dove back into work and my kids and discovered being happy "as is" again.

I still wondered what would have been between Chris and me and if any of what we had was real but I tried not to think about it too much. Our next big meeting at work was in June so I had plenty to keep my mind busy. I tried to work things out again with Dezi's dad. Huge mistake but... we learn.

As the attendees of the upcoming meeting came through our desks on the events team, curiosity got the better of me and I checked for Chris' name on the roster. It was there. He was coming to work security at the event. Shit. This is why people say not to dip your pen in the company ink! Now I have to face him and all of his buddies and my stupidity for letting him in.

Part of me was excited to see him again in some sick, perverse way. Part of me wanted to rip his eyes out and kick his dick off. But, I remained classy and calm. He would stop and try to talk to me. He'd ask me stupid questions that everyone knew the answers to, like "where's the ice machine?" I'd ignore him with every fiber of my being because I'm an Aries and that's what we do. He even emailed me a couple of times and I blew them off. We did not speak at that meeting and wouldn't. My pride wouldn't allow it. I didn't even look at him. Not once, but I wanted to.

Next event on the books for work… September in Dallas.

Again… check for his name… it's there… dammit… and also yesssssss! What the Hell is wrong with me?! My friend and I were on the ground in Dallas with a bunch of the people on our team working our tails off. Of course I knew exactly when he was arriving because I'm sick in the head over this dude still, like some love-sick teenager. But damned it, he won't know it! No one, except my best friend, who I worked with, would know it!

Fate stepped in… bless its heart. My friend and Chris' friend got put on a special project together in a car, alone. Of all of the Goddamned thousands of people there to be put on a project… it's those two. Of course, the convo ended up on what my friend knew about me and what his friend knew about him. Turned out we were *both* single again.

(To this day, Chris jokes that he thinks I set this up myself! I would've rather ripped my own arm off and beaten myself with it than to crawl back after his rejection!!)

Our friends' conversation ended up somehow with a meeting planned for us. My heart skipped a beat when I saw him and actually acknowledged him; maybe it even stopped for a few seconds. I hugged him and he smelled like heaven… it was like we were never apart, which was amazing!

I decided that I couldn't NOT forgive him and try again. I felt weak, but I was okay with that. We spent the next several weeks together, getting deeper into some sort of a relationship but never really labeling it or putting any pressure on ourselves this time. We had another great time in Dallas- unbelievably great. I wanted this more than ever but again, distance, circumstance, situations… sigh.

Back in our respective parts of the country, I was dealing with my dear friend's father passing. It was tough. She was a daddy's girl and his accident and death were very unexpected and very hard on her and her mom. We spent so much time together at his hospice care facility just waiting for the day.

I'd never lost anyone that I knew before. Her dad used to pick us up from the office and take us to lunch. We'd talk about the situation with Chris and life. He'd give us his advice and tell jokes. He was a character and was so loved. He thought I needed to move to be with Chris. That was one of the last things I remember talking to him about.

Grief does weird things to people. My friend, her boyfriend and I ended up drowning our sorrows with tequila one night, things were done, things were said and we didn't speak for a couple of weeks after that. Really, that night was the catalyst that made me realize that I wanted to be with Chris permanently with labels and location and all of that shit- no matter how complicated. Life is short.

Does This State Make Me Look Fat??

I was done with my life in Arkansas. I'd outgrown it like those jeans from high school that you kept because you thought they may fit again one day. Those bitches ain't going to fit again, face it! Yes, my whole family was there, all of my friends, my kids' lives and a job I loved. On paper it all looked great. But after a trip to visit Chris at his home in Salisbury, North Carolina, the feeling that I belonged there somehow was undeniable to me. The little voices in my head told me that I'd made mistakes before and that my kids' lives were going to be affected and what if this was a mistake and what if it didn't work out....

BUT it just felt right to move. It sounds stupid and cliché but that's really the best I can do! He could have moved to me, but his daughter was near him and he was a great father to her and didn't want to leave her. I respected that.

Chris and I did the long distance thing for awhile as I worked on logistics, each making trips on a plane and writing letters, calling multiple times daily and sending emails. Chris found an ad in his local paper for a company hiring immediately for a position just miles from his house. That ad could have been written for me. It was nearly the same exact job that I currently held but a few levels up. I interviewed with them twice over the phone and was hired, site unseen. They wanted me there as soon as possible.

"What the fuck just happened?! Am I moving? Oh my God, I'm moving!" Excitement and panic set in. Until that moment, this was a wish that may never happen. Now shit got real.

While I knew that one of my kids would benefit from getting away from the memories of his terrorist father that we hadn't spoken to in months, the other I needed to talk to, because he did put forth *some* effort. He was understandably upset but surprisingly supportive that we were planning to move away. How was that so easy?

And as a side note, that business that we both worked for when we met was Wal-Mart. I worked in corporate and he worked in the field. The store address in the town that he lived in and I was now moving to? *323* Arlington Way. No fucking way!

Things fell into place piece by piece like magic. Let's do this! I'm ready. I think.

Breaking Hearts

One of the hardest things I've ever done in my whole life was to sit down by the pool at my parents' house and tell them I got the job... and I was leaving. The day came and Chris flew in to drive us sixteen hours to North Carolina. Watching my parents, my grandparents, brother, sister-in-law and nephew in my rearview mirror as we drove off with a U-Haul headed a thousand miles away, well that moment is burned into my memory as one of the hardest days of my life.

The hardest one to leave, of course, was my mom. My mom and I are so close. She stood by me through all of this craziness. She's supported me, helped me, loved me and had given more than any one parent would ever be expected to... and then she gave more.

Don't get me wrong, I love my whole family (well, most of them), but my mom... I think we're old souls who have traveled together for centuries. She is my heart. She is my inspiration. She is my best friend. I know it tore her heart out when we left her, but for the first time in my life, I was making a decision for me too. Not solely a decision based on other peoples' needs or desires like I normally did. This was the right decision, however heartbreaking.

My two kiddos and I were off on a new adventure and life. Crazy? Looking back, yes, but I knew he was the guy for us almost immediately... all of us.

We drove eight hours to Nashville where we stayed the night and then finished the trip the next day. Chris' daughter, Maddie (who is just a few months younger than Bret) and his parents were waiting for us to get there. Maddie's first words to Bret and Dezi were "wanna play?" Of course there was an adjustment period of getting to know how to blend a family successfully and figuring out how to get around and find our place in a new city. The first year was tough. I considered going back home a few times and even started packing my clothes up one night after a heated debate.

We found that going places, doing things and being adventurous together worked like a charm. We had Chris' daughter on some weekends and we'd go on hikes or explore parks or whatever we wanted to do. It wasn't all great, but we learned how to bend with the wind and I think we were great parents to all of the kids, having family meetings and dinners and generally just enjoying life. We were good together.

We planned a huge trip to Disney World and Sea World in Orlando for the kids as a Christmas surprise. They had a blast together, riding everything and seeing things they had never seen before. We spent one night in the pool at our hotel, late into the night, just having fun together. I think sometimes the kids like those simple moments, just as much (or more) as the really elaborately planned ones.

My kiddos were making new friends and adjusting to our new life. Bret was his usually rambunctious self in class, walking around and telling jokes and pissing teachers off. He started to get more challenging the older he got. Lying more and never, ever owning up to his mistakes.

He and Chris would lie in his bed some nights and talk, I didn't know at the time about what, exactly. Chris tried to help our ten year old son as much as he could, sharing with him about maturity and trying to model responsibility for him. We both did. Nothing seemed to quite sink in. It was bothersome so we started family therapy to try to help him figure out how to handle situations both at home and in school better. At least 5 times I had teachers ask me if he'd been tested for ADHD. At least 10 times I brought it up to various doctors but no one thought he had it. We even filled out questionnaires and had teachers do the same. Nothing.

I thought that maybe the move had something to do with it so we just kept one with therapy and as much support as we could throw his way.

My Aching Ovaries

Despite the troubles with Bret, I wanted to have another baby eventually. Chris was an amazing dad and step-dad. I talked to him about it a few times and he'd say "I'm content with what we have". I don't take "no" for an answer easily when I really want something. Blame it on the stubborn Aries.

Mr. Wright and I planned a 'just the two of us' vacation to the Outer Banks while the kids were in Arkansas for the summer. I'd never seen a lighthouse before in person, even though I had started to collect them just a couple years before meeting Chris, so I was piss-my-pants excited to see and climb the Cape Hatteras lighthouse. When I saw it for the first time, it was simply breathtaking, climbing the stairs to the top, even more so (that's a lot of freaking stairs).

We had talked about marriage several times, even though I was super apprehensive about ever going back down that rabbit hole again. I sometimes wonder if humans are meant to be monogamous creatures since so many marriages end up in divorce or misery or both. I think my parents, who have miraculously been together for a fucking coon's age (something my mom says), are an anomaly.

I had a weird feeling that Chris would propose on that trip. Just me and him, beach trip, romantic setting… I waited, thinking "Ooh, this would be a perfect moment. Top of the lighthouse? Sunset on the beach? Amazing oceanside dinner?" Nothing. Not even a mention of marriage. But my feeling was so strong and they are rarely wrong. What the fuck? Maybe I was being a bit too naïve or my mind was rushing things.

One of our days there was a super rainy summer day. In our room right on the beach, while we listened to the waves crash against the shore and the rain pelt the patio outside (and after a slight miscommunication about fertility) I got my wish. I guess, in a way, Chris kind of proposed with a more unbreakable bond than a ring.

A month later, I was pleasantly surprised and so nervous to tell Chris, we brought back an unexpected souvenir, we got an engagement baby. Since he'd never really approved of my crazy idea for us to have a baby, I had no idea what to expect. We were sitting in the swing on the back porch and I was shaking, trying to find the words. They wouldn't come. In retrospect, I could have been more creative, like wrapping pick and blue baby booties up as a gift or some shit, but I wasn't quite sure how the news would be received so I finally just blurted out that I was pregnant.

After the shock wore off, Chris was excited and ended up telling people way before it was time to tell people. I wanted to wait a couple months, you know, just in case. He told everyone at work, his mom and his daughter's mom almost immediately.

Chris was a great partner during the whole pregnancy. He would tie my shoes, paint my toenails, rub my back, and attend appointments. I craved bacon like crazy so he'd bring bacon to my work almost daily. Baaaaacccccccooooooonnnn! It was as if baby took over my brain with demands of pork fat in mass quantities.

My belly was huge! People would stop me and say things like "any day now, huh?" to which I'd reply, "nope, three more months" and then I'd mutter under my breath "fuck you".

Seriously, I have a pretty wicked resting bitch face, so people didn't dare touch my belly, like they did to some of my friends… but comments people make to pregnant women are just fucked up. Here's a tip, unless your comment is "you're beautiful", just don't. Just keep walking and keep your mouth shut or risk getting karate chopped in your throat.

We (I) decided on a home birth again, which terrified Chris. I'd already had one hospital birth and one home birth and I'd pick home birth, hands down, as the best experience for me. Chris nearly worried himself into anxiety attacks, thinking the midwife wouldn't make it in time and he'd have to deliver the baby alone. I assured him I could handle it but he inadvertently wished that situation right into fruition!

I went into labor at about five in the morning and called the midwife who was an hour away. Her assistant got there just in time to catch the baby who was making her way out. I'm certain that Chris has never been happier to see another human being's face in his entire life, than when that assistant walked in the bedroom door as I was pushing like a lunatic.

I knew the baby was big, I could feel her wriggling her head as she moved down the ole' birth chute. I'd never experienced that with the other two and am happy to report I will never feel that sensation again. It was unbearable, but there I was, doing it with no other option- even though I said that I couldn't a few times in the moment.

Naturally, created on a diet of pork fat, Lana was a humongous, nine pounds, twelve ounces of squishy, "where the fuck is her neck located?" adorable baby that we all fell in love with instantly. We integrated her right into out lives as best we could; taking her along with us as we did the older kids. Chris and Lana were immediately inseparable. She may as well have popped out with an "I'm a daddy's girl" onesie on.

When we had Lana, I just could not fathom putting her in daycare like I had to with Dezi. I would research daycares near us while pregnant and break into hormonal fits of tears immediately. It made me sick to my stomach. I was determined to find a better way, so I did. Once I weeded through the "work from home bullshit", I found two viable options: 1. Event business for weddings and parties or 2. A virtual assistant business.

Since we were dead in the middle of a recession and events weren't in huge demand at that time, my decision was made. I'd start a virtual assistant and consulting business where I could work from home with the new baby.

I started my business a few months before she was born and had enough of a clientele once she arrived to visit my boss during my maternity leave and quit. It was one of the greatest decisions of my life to be able to be mom when the kids needed me and not have to ask permission to go to games or lunches or appointments.

Like I'd Dreamed it Would Be

We went on a family vacation, to the same beach hotel that Lana decided to join our family in over a year prior. All four of our kiddos were there with us, exploring the Outer Banks, splashing in the water and collecting seashells. Chris took me to my favorite lighthouse with all four of our kids and got down on one knee and asked me to marry him. In my mind, I already was so… no brainer there.

We were married in a perfect ceremony with just the two of us on the beach of Trunk Bay in the Virgin Islands. It was awesome. After we were officially announced husband and wife (which was kinda lame because it was just us and the officiate) a stingray swam by us a few feet away. We were official and I became Mrs. Wright.

Then we ate peanut butter and jelly sandwiches for our wedding night dinner because we waited too late to go out. We made up for it the next night, after we got super sunburned while snorkeling though. It was a grand adventure that felt official.

There was a seven year age gap between our baby and my daughter, Dezi. Driving around, having a couples' day on a Black Friday, we were throwing the idea around that it may be awesome to have a little playmate for Lana. Before we could change our minds (not that we would have) our second baby (collective kiddo numero cinco) was underway. We were all excited but, that excitement didn't get to stick around too long before our attention was diverted.

There we were, with the fresh news of our new pregnancy on our minds, sitting across from a police officer in my son's high school. This was not the first time he was in trouble recently, even though we had been in therapy and tried every trick in the book. He was what I like to call my "Robin Williams" kid, as our therapist called him. Always making people laugh in class- showing off, being silly. I got phone calls from teachers- practically since the kid could talk.

But this was the first time he was in REAL trouble. He had been charged with a false report of mass violence on school property. He was being charged with a juvenile felony.

I cried like I've never cried for him that day. I called my mom, barely able to get the words out. Would this be on his permanent record? Would he still be able to go to school? What kind of a mother must I be to have a kid who does things like this?

It was really the start of our downward spiral, both as individuals and as a family. It was our descent into a Hell that I don't wish on any mother... ever. I can't watch stories on the news anymore that share troubled kids, or even adults, and NOT feel for their mothers.

I wish we... or I, could have done things better. That I could have done something differently somehow... retrospect is a bitch. But looking back, I truly feel that I did everything in my power and at some point, kids have to accept responsibility for their actions. It was time for me to step back a bit and let natural consequence take its toll. It was so hard to fight biology and not try to jump in to his rescue.

Court dates, attorney appointments, schooling decisions, community service, state mandated family therapy, probation officers and midwife meetings. Fucking fabulous. It's not that I wasn't happy that we were having another baby, but the timing was fucked and the head of the Mom Guilt Posse' started talking shit in my head:

"Who are you to have ANOTHER baby? You can't even handle the kids you have. Look at you! You're a shitty mother, obviously, or your kid wouldn't even be in this position."

"Oh God! What in the fuck am I doing? I can't do this. I can't!" And then I'd cry. And throw up. And eat some Wavy Lays with French onion dip and some apples with peanut butter and all would be right in the world for a minute.

We made it through somehow, step by step. Intensive therapy, talking and working through the shit. I didn't really know it at the time but this was the start of my own sinking into a black hole. It seemed like we'd take a few steps forward and a few steps back- never really making progress but always hoping for it when we saw a shimmer of light.

My son and Chris (his stepdad) really started pulling apart at this point, which put me and my huge belly right in the middle of their intense arguments. I wanted to take my son's side. I wanted to agree with my husband too. There was no winning for me. Either way, I fucking lose.

Things with Chris and I started unraveling at this point too. We argued a lot- mostly about Bret. A couple can only take so much tension and so much change and so much attention diverted in 47,000 different directions, before foundations crack. I didn't know what to do so I just started shutting down. I still managed to stand before a judge in a crowded courtroom (I only THOUGHT I had social anxiety before) and testify for my kid, unable to see my toes and due to pop out a new baby anytime.

Undoubtedly that was one of the most embarrassing moments in my life.

I could feel the judgment, not on my son, but on me as a mother, "pregnant again when she can't even control this one". The voices in my head were there, loud and clear of what people must be thinking of me. And this time it wasn't imaginary. It was real.

Dark, Dark, Dark

At a point in my life when I should have been excited about a new baby, shopping for booties, assembling nursery furniture and enjoying our family and our kids, I had started mentally contemplating suicide and crying daily… and no one had a clue. I was a master at hiding my depression. During this pregnancy, I started feeling very anxious, nervous, depressed and alone. Knowing what I know now, I can definitely see that there were some massive issues sneaking in there, pregnancy related or not. I never really told a soul because I feel comfortable as "the strong one" who does the helping but never asks for help myself.

Some people don't know about my mental black hole to this day and won't unless they read this book. That's how well I hide things. I tried to share with Chris but by that time we were ass-deep in moving into our new house we'd just bought and Bret's stuff and just LIFE, so I think he passed it off as pregnancy and situational emotion. I was always upbeat and happy on the outside but on the inside, dark, dark, dark.

While my mother and father-in-law took the older kids to the beach (my in-laws are absolutely incredible people and I'm certain we'd already be divorced if not for them), I went into labor early in the morning. With a midwife assistant present right at the moment I was pushing (the midwife didn't make this one either… sorry Chris). This delivery was easy, after the previous nearly ten pound linebacker baby. I must have an elasta-vag by now!

Our newest little lady made her appearance in the wee hours of an August morning. She was born perfect and amazing. How poetic that my first baby and my last baby weighed exactly the same- eight pounds, ten ounces.

We were getting used to our new family of seven. We had my two older kids in the house, my husband's daughter who lived with her momma about an hour away, our then three year old together and now this new little nugget. I had a renewed hope in what could be in our future. That the feelings and thoughts I was having would subside now. That hope was short lived.

Again, my in-laws were in town for the weekend so, like I sometimes do, I took advantage of the extra set of hands and headed out for a long overdue hair appointment and a bit of Christmas shopping for a couple of hours alone.

There is no sigh of relief like the one that you have when you get actual ALONE time. When you can breathe and not have to wipe anyone's nose or ass or listen to the word "moooooooooooommmmmmmmmmmmyyyyyyy" for a few hours. This feeling is a lot like what I think Heaven must feel like.

I was in Kohls, looking at a cute little dress to wear to hubby's company Christmas party that night, when my phone rang. It was Chris, he was probably going to ask something stupid like 'where are the baby wipes' or 'how long do we heat up the breast milk'. I will never, ever forget the feeling that came over me on that phone call, ever, when he instead asked me "did you move my gun"?

I thought he was joking at first.

My husband is many things: kind, funny, hard working, considerate and absolutely ANAL about his things being moved. I can go into the garage and move one tool from his toolbox and the man will know which tool is missing and in exactly the space that that motherfucker belongs, in a matter of hours. It's that last quality about him that I will now FOREVER be grateful for, for the rest of my life.

His gun is always put away. It's not in a place that anyone could accidentally run across it, unless they are looking for it. And someone was.

"No, I didn't move your gun, what do you mean? Are you kidding right now, because it is not funny." I snapped, half hoping he was joking and half knowing that he wasn't.

"Let me call you back" he said. And he hung up the phone. I dropped everything that I had in my hands and made my way toward the door.

My life has never been in slower motion than it was in that moment. I could not drive fast enough, pray hard enough or get to my son to tell him that everything was going to be okay. I knew exactly where that once hidden gun had disappeared to, and my mind went to places in that 10 minutes that I hope it will never have to go to again.

I pictured my 16 year old son (who was pissed off about being grounded) with a deadly weapon in a house with a stepdad he no longer liked and a depression he felt compelled to act on.

I called as many times as my phone would let me, redialing like someone desperate to win a radio contest, but no one answered. I finally reached my driveway after what seemed like a decade. There were police there, I was frantic. Everyone was out of the house except my husband and the cops. I walked in and the cops went upstairs into my son's room.

I was waiting for something, anything. Hysterical doesn't even come close to the feeling I was feeling inside. I had no control.

"Please, God don't let there be a gunshot." I sat alone. As minutes that felt like hours passed, I finally saw my son's beautiful face coming down the stairs with the police. He was in handcuffs and his eyes looked empty and out of hope. His face was tear-soaked and I wanted to hold him close to me and shut out the world like I did the morning he was born. The officer put his finger to his lips and motioned for me to not say anything. I had to fight every fiber of my being to remain quiet and composed.

That was MY son. My gorgeous baby boy that I had made promises to that I'd never let anything happen to him. The one I'd pumped pieces of my soul into, the one I had loved with my entire heart for 16 years, and he was being taken to the hospital for attempted suicide. He'd already written the letter. He had no regard for his own life any longer and had given up all hope.

I had failed as a parent. But how?

How did I give up everything to BE everything for him and nearly lose him? How could I be such a monumental, piece of shit mother that I can't even raise a kid who wants the most basic, human desire of life? The self hating voices wouldn't stop.

I tanked in that moment. A part of my heart died forever and I'm not sure I will ever fully recover from that day.

I had to wait to see him. I couldn't go that night, as much as I needed to. He was "getting settled" they said, and I could see him tomorrow. I sat in the living room shocked, terrified and devastated… but grateful he was alive. I had to try to hold it together for my little ones. In our conversation later, my husband brought up the fact that, in a matter of hours, we were due to be at a Christmas party.

"Are you fucking kidding? No. Go without me. I just want to lay in bed and cry, Chris." I said.

The anger set in. "How could he even ask me to go to some stupid social event when my son was in such turmoil? Selfish asshole." I thought to myself.

But then, my mother-in-law, my mom and my own self preservation kicked me in the ass. I somehow composed myself and went to that party and I downed more Crown and Cokes than usual that night. I'm sure my liver thanks me. I think that's the first moment that The Drunk Mom came to be, even though I didn't really know it yet. I had to unwind and process.

The Drunk Mom is Born

My mind was a blabbering, self loathing, dagger throwing mess for the next several weeks... no, months. Not only were the Mom Guilt Posse' in my head just LOVING this new situation in which to completely trash me as a human, mom, wife, sister, aunt, daughter, granddaughter and all things that one could ever possibly be... but also, there was another tiny level of self understanding that started happening for me- tiny, but there.

That understanding went something like "you tried so hard to be perfect, do perfect, have perfect... look what that got you?!" It was a tiny "aha" moment in a slew of more to come. I learned a ton about judging other people, other parents and being a 'real human being' going forward- not hiding my mistakes or shortcomings or feelings as a person.

I got to go to the hospital to see Bret. I went every single day and called to check on his status in between visits. He was in a "padded holding room" at the local hospital until a bed opened up at a mental facility where he would be admitted. We had no options. He was there "until" he could get help.

I didn't realize until this incident, that mental hospitals are full to the brim and there are frequently times where there are no beds available within many miles of a patient. Mentally ill people sit in waiting, in little rooms with beds on the floor, TV's encased in plastic boxes mounted to the ceiling and staff that watches patients in their rooms with camera systems 24/7, so that no one tries to off themselves with a bed sheet.

My once vibrant, funny, loving son lay emotionless, curled up in a little ball in his hospital gown as I tried to talk to him. He seemed so frail. He said nothing at first. He wouldn't even look at me. I just held him and told him that everything was going to be okay and that I'd be right here for him and I loved him. I must have said "I love you 27,000 times in that first visit". I've never wanted someone to REALLY HEAR THAT more. He finally looked at me and cried. We cried together.

We waited for a bed for I think four or five days (all of my days kind of ran together at that point). I checked in as usual to get my name badge and be buzzed into his secure area. The receptionist said "we don't have a patient by that name here."

I gave her the name again, spelled it, gave her the room number and pointed to exactly where he was. My path was memorized by now.

"I'm sorry, he's been checked out." Bitch said (I'm sure she's a lovely lady, but in the moment, when someone says their facility has essentially fucking LOST your kid... yeah, we'll refer to her as Bitch)

"Bitch, what?" I thought.

"He can't be checked out" I said "I'm his mother, he's a minor child and I didn't get a phone call, so he has to be here." My voice elevated.

"Ma'am I'm sorry, the computer says he's been checked out and that's all of the information I have." Bitch says.

This is not something I recommend anyone ever telling a mother... ever... unless they want the tongue lashing of a lifetime and the risk of being physically maimed.

I went to visit my son and he was gone. No one could tell me where he was, when he left... nadda. To say I was livid? Yeah... multiply that by 10,000, add in lots of F-bombs and let's go with that to describe my reaction in this moment.

I finally got some little office twit to come explain to me that they had transferred Bret to xyz facility at xyz time (which was minutes before I arrived) and I could visit him the following day. Turns out that a bed opened up at a facility about an hour away, so they transferred my kid right then, no phone call for mom.

No "hey, we know you've been through Hell recently as a parent, but we just want to give you a heads-up on the creature that you carried for nine months, squeezed out of your vaj-hole and nurtured for 16 motherfucking years…. Yeah, we're moving him to xyz facility now."

Nothing.

I cried so hard in my car in the parking garage, I think people thought that *I* was the mental patient. They weren't far off in their assumption but we'll talk about that later.

Now, I know that there are times in everyone's life when God or Baby Jesus, or whatever you believe in (I prefer Captain Universe) throws you some challenges… Curveballs… Bumps in the road to see how you'll handle situations or teach you some grand lesson.

This is a point in my life where I cussed out Captain U from the lower level of a parking garage like you have probably never heard.

"How much can one person REALLY FUCKING take U?! What did we do, what did I do to deserve this?!"

I was physically shaking and traumatized by all that we'd been through and this was the icing on the cake. I was heading for a breakdown… so I called my mom and bawled like a baby, getting about every other word out and my voice shaking.

I've always been extremely conscious of my parents being amazing gifts in my life. They have truly been one of the reasons I hold on in the rough times, more than they will ever know.

My dad arranged for my mom to fly in, in a few days to be with me, see Bret and help where she could with the younger kids. My mom has been Bret's best friend since day one. He was her first grandchild. She has never wavered in her support for him and like me, has probably over-compensated a wee bit too.

My dad had to work and could only send my mom at the moment so I looked forward to seeing her in just a couple of days. I really needed a hug from my mommy. I was busy doing things around the house and there was a knock at my door. Usually knocks at the door are religious recruiters or people selling me a miracle cleaning agent that they simply must show me on my front door (I let them show me because that's the only time my front door gets cleaned!).

This time I saw a short man with dirty blonde hair at my door. I was in shock. It was my dad! He'd secretly flown in and rented a car to get to my house. My knees buckled a bit and I wept like a little three year old who had just skinned her knee (or more likely had both of her legs being run through a meat grinder). I wrapped my arms around him and sobbed.

I'm a damned good writer, but I will never be able to articulate to you what it meant to have both my mom and my dad at my side when I needed them, when we needed them, the most.

We drove an hour to Charlotte to pick my mom up and then another two hours to Greensboro to see Bret in his new facility. Same deal- strict security, no clothing with drawstrings, no children allowed to visit, no purses, pens, belts. Nothing anyone could harm themselves with. Two people at a time, limited time, beds low to the ground with no place to tie anything.

He was in therapy several times a day, being medicated with multiple types of medicine. He was diagnosed with several issues, one of which was Oppositional Defiant Disorder. A few times when we visited him he was not himself at all- like a zombie. It was the medicine. Medicine that I later learned would cost over $400 a month and that he would refuse once we got him checked out and back home. I offered supplements, alternate therapy, more counseling. He resisted so we did things his way. What choice did I have? You diagnose a kid with ODD (meaning he defies authority) and then you (the authority) tell him to take his medicine. Anyone else see the irony here?

I Love You... But Get Out

Teenagers can be tough. Teens with strong personalities are tougher. Teens with all that going on plus depression, ODD and ADHD are a fucking nightmare, especially when you have younger kids who are seeing every single thing that goes on, even when you're trying your damndest to hide it.

There are several theories about what causes these conditions. Truth is that I had properly identified the ADHD and ODD in him, by myself, before all of this happened. I personally believe that there is a connection between what he went through with his father at such a young age and what happened IN him as a result. But what do I know? I'm just his mom who read books and scoured the internet and hired therapists and asked medical doctors for reasons and solutions... unsuccessfully.

But I still loved him. Of course! He's still my boy, my oldest, my heart and soul... but seriously, at one point our conversation ended in me saying "if you can't follow our rules here get out of the nest, dude". He thought his way was always right, I knew nothing, anything we asked him to do; he did the opposite, anything we asked him NOT to do; he did it.

He would smoke pot IN his bedroom upstairs. It smelled like Willy Nelson's tour bus up there. I'd go up to confront him and he'd act like I was totally nuts through his droopy, red eyes. Nobody needs that much Visine for "allergy eyes" in their medicine cabinet AND in their car, especially when they don't suffer from allergies. Like I wasn't raised by redneck-hippies and I didn't know *that* smell like it was household incense growing up!? Come on!

Jesus, the arguments we'd have. The tension in our house! I could write the rest of this book with chapters filled with nothing but shenanigans and bullshit but I'll spare you. Things came to a point where I had to make a decision about what was best for everyone in our family. Not just Bret, not just the other kids but everyone. My dad had volunteered several times to let Bret come live with him on his job site in North Dakota. For many reasons, I decided yes. Now was the time.

I bought my son a one way ticket on an airplane to live 2000 miles away from me. That trip to the airport sucked. Part of me felt like I was letting him down or that I was giving up. Why are there no decisions that are just easy with this kid?! Shit! He lived with my dad in a fairly desolate place where hopefully, he'd have an opportunity to grow up a little bit and take his schooling online and stay out of trouble.

Things were calming down around the house, Chris and I were slowly reconnecting, I was able to refocus my attention on the girls and my business and we were checking in on Bret daily. Life was almost normal again, or as normal as it would ever be with kids and bills and ya know… stuff.

There were minor issues between my dad and Bret but nothing terrible. Things we could deal with. We were moving closer to adulthood, that magical age of eighteen that kids think will make everything so awesome and life will begin and "I can do what I want".

I, too, thought there would be this sigh of relief at my child's adulthood, this goal point of crossing some sort of imaginary finish line and brushing my hands together, taking a bow for a job well done… or at least, finished.

Welp, I hate to tell you, that moment never came. I'm still waiting, still worried about him, still think about him daily, still hope he makes good choices and becomes a man he can be proud to be. The difference now is that he's out there on his own and I can't watch over him or try to control anything in his life anymore, which is the catch to having adult kids.

I can't say that those feelings will ever end. Maybe that's the trap of parenthood. We race toward a finish line that doesn't exist and then we wish we hadn't raced so hard once we get to where we thought that stupid fucking finish line would be. I don't know.

The depression was now in full force for me after some other losses too painful to share with anyone, so I scheduled a month long trip at my mom and dad's place for the girls and I… to try to gather myself and find support. Truthfully, I needed a break from marriage and life and this was as close as I'd ever get without becoming a gypsy or a carnie. It helped a little bit.

On the trip to my mom and dad's farm, I made some life decisions. There's a place on their property where I grew up, that I just find fucking magical. It's at the top of their hill, overlooking the beauty of the Ozarks where sunsets are gorgeous, the wind blows through your hair and the grass sways. Poetic... ain't it? If you're lucky, you'll see some deer run past. It's amazing and I go there in my mind frequently.

In that place, I was contemplating my future, my direction. The business I had been building since 2009 wasn't as successful as I wanted it to be, even though I had busted my ass for nearly seven years and invested thousands and thousands of dollars into it. It was because I built that business out of necessity, not passion. I didn't really WANT to be doing that work day in and day out for the rest of my life anymore. Not when I really dug down deep.

That was a tough realization for me, considering all that I put into it. Could I really just drop it? And for what? "What do you really want then, Amy?" I asked myself. The answer never came. But I knew my current business was going to be ending soon, either way, even though it was my only source of income.

A few weeks later, back home in my garage, I was tinkering with some Pinterest projects, having a few drinks, having fun. The idea for The Drunk Mom struck! I immediately told my husband "I think this could be really funny to have a few drinks, do some Pinterest projects, talk about mom life, tell some jokes and really just let it all out and swear and be real... uncensored"

"You don't want to do that." He said. "Our kids are going to see that and you don't want to put yourself out there in that way."

So I put the idea on the back burner and returned to my project.

My New Mantra for Everything

June 28th, 2016, I was in the laundry room, folding sheets. "Why does anyone fold fitted sheets?" I wondered. "This would be a funny video if I was attempting to fold one of these stupid things while having a drink...or three."

I dragged my little $5 phone holder out, mounted it to the laundry room cabinet and made that video right then, on a whim. I also created a Facebook page with The Drunk Mom title, just like my husband said I shouldn't. I also bought www.thedrunkmom.com because Godammit I was going to put a website up one day too.

I posted that video and made a couple others with a few people watching in those first couple of days. Fear kicked in, those stupid voices whispered in my mind "you don't want to embarrass your kids or your family".

But this time, those voices in my head were met with a rebuttal and that rebuttal was like the closing argument in the case of the century, from the most badass, female defense attorney on the face of the Earth... no, the Universe.

She said:

"Amy, YOU HAVE DONE EVERYTHING as best as you possibly could for your kids, especially your son. You didn't get drunk around him, or do things to embarrass him, you baked the goddamned cookies for class instead of buying them (most of the time), and you attended every school concert, game, parent/teacher conference and then some. You busted your ass so that they could have name brand stuff. You took the "normal path" in jobs that you hated and never really had an opportunity or guts to follow what YOU wanted... and look where we ended up, my dear. Look what path your son chose, still. Even with all of your effort. And look at how miserable you are now.

Why not do something that you love that scares the shit out of you and challenges the status quo and asks "why" of gender rules and makes people feel like they aren't alone and that they are normal and something that makes them laugh too?

And don't you want YOUR kids to do what makes them happy, regardless of what other people think of them? Don't you want them to follow their hearts and live with moxie and shine bright? Don't you want to be THAT person for your kids?

Your gift is humor, use it. Be THAT girl. Be The Drunk Mom."

Man… that bitch is gooooooood.

I decided right then to stop following, like I had been doing for so long, and start leading. To go rogue and to be the person that I wanted to be, doing what I wanted to do despite what all of the gurus said was right. Moms aren't supposed to swear and drink and share their feelings of inadequacy and shortcomings and things that make them feel bad. Business women aren't supposed to get so personal and put everything out there for the public to see. They might lose customers.

I no longer gave one single fuck. I was tired of hiding and filtering and pretending that life came in a neat little, well organized box. It does not. It spills out of the box that is sometimes collapsing under the weight of everything it has to hold and it oozes all over and is messy and shitty and sometimes a little bit (or a lotta bit) fucked up.

Done. No fucks given to anyone else's opinions or objections or rebuttals on what I was or was not doing with *my* life.

"Fuck it." I said to myself while shrugging my shoulders. It was my new motto. FUCK IT.

So, I wrote out a whole list of jokes that I thought were funny. I sat down one day in my glamorous laundry room, against the brick wall as a backdrop (because that place has the best natural light EVER) and recorded several videos, edited them, wondered if people would think they were as funny as I did, and went for it. All in.

I made a goal of a thousand Facebook Page likes in a month. But instead, in a matter of a month, I'd hit something like six thousand. To put that in perspective, I'd worked on my business page for five years and only had about twelve-hundred likes. Kind of a big deal!

I also started doing live feeds in Facebook where I could be funny unscripted and engage with people more. My friend, Share Ross, actually suggested it, because she's a genius. It terrified me. What if I wasn't funny or witty or said something stupid while people were watching live? I can't edit that!

"Fuck it." I said to myself again, this time almost subconsciously.

I got an idea about doing something around the perception of perfection. I'd share the story about how I shit my pants while on a business trip, driving in downtown DC with a stomach virus to prove my point. No one shares their crap moments (literally and figuratively) on social media! We share the edited ones where your family is all clean and wearing matching white dresses and suits. And the hair bows that match perfectly with the boy's ties that you made by hand from Pinterest. That's not real life, that's filtered life, which we're all really great at showing online.

"Oh God, am I really going to share my horror story about shitting my pants in a rental car that will, likely, never smell the same again?" I thought.

I almost didn't hit the go button. My kids were home, they would be noisy and probably interrupt the feed, especially my wild-ass three year old, who throws a tantrum at least 6 times a day over really important things, like her banana not being peeled right, or a blanket touching her foot or insisting on wearing snow boots in the middle of a 100 degree day.

I'd look "unprofessional" and silly.

"Yep… you'll look unprofessional and silly… and that, my dear bitch, is the point here. Hit the button". My new-found power voice said. "Fuck it!"

So, I proceeded to do what any woman who needs five minutes free of little people clinging to her do… I told my thirteen year old that she was in charge for a few minutes, I locked myself in the bathroom and I hit the "go live" button.

Holy Balls!

That video, my first ever Drunk Mom Live video, went bananas (correctly peeled bananas). People were liking and loving and sharing and commenting like nothing I had ever seen first hand. People were thanking me and saying that that one short, honest moment in my bathroom, changed their life and made them feel normal. And it changed mine too.

How is it that I spent seven years trying to change people's lives and worked SO HARD at it, but never really got to where I wanted to be in my "serious business"? But talking about shitting myself while locked in my bathroom while my toddler is beating down the door behind me... that changes lives and goes viral?! And... it's so much easier.

In that moment, I learned that passion fueled dreams are easier. Notice I said easy-ER. Still effort, still work, but hot damn the results are one hundred times my effort in this project. Why? Because I fucking love it and want to tell people about it and could make videos every day in some form or another.

Everything I published from that point on was well received. I was getting several hundred likes daily, messages from people all over the world and comments about how much people loved my style of brutal, honest comedy.

That one video "The Time I Shit My Pants and Imperfection" reached the desk of a producer for a new talk show in L.A. She sent me a message on my Facebook page on a Thursday afternoon, inviting me to come to Los Angeles, all expenses paid.

At first I was wondering if it was legit, of course so I called to find out. The lady was super nice and said she'd seen my "shit my pants" video and many others and would love to hear more about my story. So I told her a tiny part of what I've just told you.

She wanted to consult with the executive producers and let me know, but the show taped that Tuesday so they'd want to fly me out on Monday… that's in just a few days! I have three girls at home and a husband who works tons of hours!

By Saturday night, I had a plane ticket for Los Angeles, a room booked, transportation arranged for me and we were off to the races!

The show was a new venture by Bishop T.D. Jakes, which if you follow Oprah at all, you'd probably recognize him. His show had just been picked up by OWN that week. I was going to be on OWN!! Talk about a dream coming true!

I arrived in L.A. and had a man in a suit holding a sign with my name on it. My driver! I hopped into the back of the Lexus and we drove what could not have been more than fifteen miles in an hour and fifteen minutes! The traffic was insane. I thought it was fun that some people were trying to see in my window to see if I was someone famous.

The morning of taping I felt great. Not as nervous as I had been the previous three days. I had a driver to the studio too. There were already people lined up outside when we arrived. There was a lot of security at the studio, and more trailers than an Arkansas trailer park, but maybe a bit fancier.

I started with hair, which was awesome.

He asked "how do you normally wear your hair?"
I said "rarely washed and in a ponytail".

He laughed. It was probably the first time an actual curling iron has touched my hair in a good five years. He teased and sprayed and curled. I asked if I could take him home. He laughed again.

Next up was makeup. I already had makeup on but she wanted to "touch up". I got a full mask, baby, and an airbrushed one. She made my eyes look like I was a model. The best part was the fake eyelashes. I've never worn fake eyelashes because, well, toddlers like to pull on things and just… no.

I looked like a goddamned rock star. I also asked the makeup artist to come home with me so she could make me look presentable in the car rider line. She also had to cover up the tattoo on my foot because it was exposed and they were a "conservative show". Ummmm, hello? The Drunk Mom here!

The experience was amazing and now I'm awaiting my call from Oprah and Ellen and a huge book deal and speaking gigs and people who want to throw money at me ☺ It showed me what is possible for a teen mom with a burning desire. Anything.

Anytime you reach the masses, you will meet resistance… and trolls, lots and lots of trolls. For someone like me, who was terrified of what people thought of me even walking into a room, you can imagine my horror when I finally conquered that fear and put myself out there… like really out there, and people started posting criticism and meanness and pure douchebaggery. Some of the comments on my videos were gross and mean and hateful:

"I'll never get that four minutes of my life back"

"I'd lick your ass"

"That was stupid"

"You just lost me as a follower"

"You're a pathetic excuse for a mother"

At first, it was heartbreaking and every time I'd see them my heart would race and I'd try to decide if I should come up with a rebuttal or block or delete…

Then I decided to use my own philosophy… laughter. Laugh because these are just people who are likely miserable or jealous or threatened or just angry at the world. Sometimes I do have a witty comment for them, right before I block them, but now I'm learning to not engage with the negative energy and just move on.

The Drunk Mom page grew to over thirty thousand fans in four months.

My Why

The Drunk Mom started as an outlet for me, a creative way to express my gift of humor and make people laugh and to re-direct my depressed, anxiety filled energy somewhere positive. But I learned really quickly that it's much bigger than that. I've gotten so many amazing messages and emails and comments. Those are where I focus my energy. Those are my why

"I am a soldier and I started watching you on a 24 hour duty (anything for a laugh to stay awake) then after watching multiple video posts I realized you are living the life! I wish I wasn't working EVERY TIME you go live. I wish I could have more time with my boys. You have great incite, please keep it coming. It's not just the laughs; it's the real sense of being that you have that makes a difference."

"Your posts get me through these moments. I'm grateful I'm not alone. And you show me that and you're not ashamed!!!"

"So I've gotta say you are my hero! You say and show all the things I feel everyday of my life! Messy cars (that was my favorite it inspired me to clean out all the random shit from my back seat followed by a few threats to keep it cleanER.....) temper tantrums, stupid shit you do with your husband to stay entertained, the list goes on and on. Any ways my real purpose in this message was to tell you thank you."

"Thank you for doing what you're doing and saying the things that others desperately need to hear. Your short video pulled my heart strings today. Usually you can just put a smile on my face and let me know I'm doing okay."

"I'm expecting! The Drunk Mom really helped shift my aversion to motherhood ... and now I'm thrilled to be in biz for myself and my baby and budding family"

How on EARTH could I dream of quitting with all of these amazing letters that come in daily?

So I did what any logical person would do… I quit my business, yeah… the business that was paying my bills. Irresponsible? Maybe. But I quit because it no longer made me happy. In fact, it was making me physically sick every time I "went to work" in the mornings. That visceral reaction to the business that I had built was all that I needed to know about the future of that venture. I was done. I let all of my contracts with clients expire, not knowing what was next or how we'd make it or if this Drunk Mom thing would ever pan out.

I had to make room for book deals, sponsors, speaking, live events, TDM weekend retreats… it's all there. I don't know when and I don't know exactly how but I do know it's on its way to me.

I have so much faith. Faith that there is NO POSSIBLE WAY that something that has been this successful in such a short period of time, that is positively affecting so many lives, that is bringing me so much happiness, can be wrong and can NOT catch fire even more.

Just the Beginning

In the first three months of this adventure, I created over 30 videos, added thirty thousand followers on my page, had been interviewed by a network talk show and had been viewed by several million people across the world. THREE MONTHS.

This isn't to brag and say "look how awesome I am". This is to show you what is possible for you.

Remember, I was the teen mom, destined for failure and mediocrity. I was the young wife who had her head screwed up by her abusive husband. I was the young lady who made many mistakes and learned from all of them. I was the woman who started and worked in a business for seven years that ultimately failed (failure is really a good thing!). I was the woman whose husband discouraged her idea and who did it anyway on a hunch. I am the woman who is working every day to make this world more funny and more accepting. I am the woman who is making people feel better about the way their car looks or the fact that their kids too, are sometimes assholes. I am the woman who battles depression with my comedy every single day of my life and who still sometimes has suicidal tendencies, despite my best efforts to "just be happy".

You have stories too. You have hardships and losses and fears too. We all do because of this human condition we've found ourselves in. Those very things can be your undoing or they can be your catalysts. You can wallow in self pity, which I still do at least once or twice a month, or not. You could be on the verge of your big idea or already have your idea but people are telling you not to. Or you could be scared shitless of putting yourself out there, of getting on that dance floor, or making that video.

BUT... you could be three months from your massive breakthrough. You could be three days from your talk show appearance or a book deal or a multi-million dollar contract. Who knows?

You can freakin' snap and throw your hands up and take a long drive off of a short pier or you can snap and embrace what life is right now, messy, imperfect and crazy… and live the fuck out of it in this moment, as is.

Fuck it.

You get to choose who you want to be. I'm The Drunk Mom. Who do you want to be?

Do you love The Drunk Mom?

Support the ongoing work of TDM, spreading this mission for moms
all over the world, by becoming a behind the scenes member
(means you're going to get special shit that other people don't get)

www.Patreon.com/TheDrunkMom

Book Bonuses

For access to hidden videos, pictures and other fun stuff go to

www.TheDrunkMom.com/BecomingTheDrunkMom